Hope:
THE STRONGEST MOTIVATION

MICHAEL E. PAYTON, MA

authorHOUSE®

AuthorHouse™
1663 Liberty Drive
Bloomington, IN 47403
www.authorhouse.com
Phone: 833-262-8899

Published by AuthorHouse 02/19/2021

ISBN: 978-1-6655-1756-0 (sc)
ISBN: 978-1-6655-1755-3 (e)

Library of Congress Control Number: 2021903566

Print information available on the last page.

Any people depicted in stock imagery provided by Getty Images are models,
and such images are being used for illustrative purposes only.
Certain stock imagery © *Getty Images.*

This book is printed on acid-free paper.

Scripture quotations marked KJV are from the Holy Bible, King James Version
(Authorized Version). First published in 1611. Quoted from the KJV Classic
Reference Bible, Copyright © *1983 by The Zondervan Corporation.*

This book is dedicated to four individuals who have played invaluable roles in both Vicki and my lives: our parents.
Mr. and Mrs. Eugene R. Payton
Mr. and Mrs. James Thomas Seth, Sr.

It is Vicki and my HOPE that we have channeled our lives in the direction that you intended.
God Bless!

ABOUT THE COVER

I've always believed that hope is certainly seen through the eyes of children more frequently and more intensely than anywhere else. Children have nonconditional hope and innocence. In their eyes and hearts anything is possible, there is no petty jealousies, cheating or hate. Children have the hope of great things not only in their lives but the lives of all that our world will prosper in bringing joy and great health to all without prejudice or abuse. It is a hope we should all learn from.

Michael E. Payton, MA

FOREWORD

As with my two previous books, "Just for Thought-Articles of Motivation," and "Time to Think-Meditation and Reflection," the theme here is indeed motivation.

The Holy Bible is certainly a motivational and inspirational resource for Christians as well as non-Christians. There can be no doubt that regardless of religious persuasion both the Old and the New Testament leave the reader thinking. Certainly, there are many who try to delegitimize the content while many of us believe it to be God's word. Either belief has one common element: The Bible leaves everyone who reads it thinking and that in itself has motivated each reader to try to prove or disprove.

What I wanted to do with this book was not to critique the Bible but rather to take many of the motivational and inspirational quotes throughout and relate them in a modern-day methodology. I wanted to show individuals that many of the motivational techniques and principles used today for inspiring individuals, students, families, and businesses are, to say the least, time tested.

It is my hope that as you read "Hope: the Strongest Motivation," that hope indeed is the strongest form of motivation in your life. History is full of many stories of famine, war, destruction, and senseless killings. The question becomes, 'what keeps people going, moving forward in life?' Could the answer to that age-long question be, "Hope"?

This book leaves the answer to that question totally up to you. What this book does do is make you think. It is my hope the book will show you how these motivational techniques were applied throughout the centuries to many problems we today couldn't even comprehend and possibly give the readers some ideas to use in motivating their own lives.

I would finally add that this project has been inspiring and motivating to me in ways other books and projects I've been involved never did.

Writing this book has given me the opportunity to read and outline the Bible in ways I never would have otherwise.

Writing "Hope: The Strongest Motivation," has indeed been both inspirational and motivational for me and my "Hope" for you is that somewhere in your life you will find it beneficial.

CONTENTS

THE OLD TESTAMENT

THE NEW TESTAMENT

The Old Testament

CHAPTER 1

Genesis *"I Got Your Back"*

"And behold, I am with thee and will keep thee in all places
whither thou goest...I will not leave thee..." Genesis 28:15

THERE IS A PHRASE, "I got your back." Normally you hear that phrase among friends where one tells the other, he can always depend on him.

It's always reassuring to know you have someone looking out for you. As children growing up our parents were there for us. If we got in trouble or had a problem most of us were fortunate enough to have one or both to go to for help.

Then some of us also had our brothers or sisters when things got tense. Also, our really best friends were ready to stand by our side if needed.

In reciprocating, you were always there to have these same people's backs whenever a situation arose.

So, what inspires this intense loyalty and dedication to others? In some cases, it's the "family thing." Relatives take care of relatives. Friendships and other "bonding "relationships spawn the loyalty for non-relatives: Friends take care of friends.

The question now: who is there for you anytime? Do you have a family member or friend who really has your back? An additional question is: do you have that person's back in the same manner?

Christians today know as they always have, that just like Genesis 28:15 makes very clear, God has our back.

CHAPTER 2

Exodus *"Honor Your Father and Your Mother"*

*"Honor your father and your mother, that your days may be prolonged
in the land which the Lord your God gives you." Exodus 20:12*

T HE TWO PEOPLE I MISS most in my life are my mom and dad. I'm
reasonably certain most of you feel the same way about your parents
if they have passed.

I am very aware of the conflicts many children have with their
parents, conflicts which never ended until the parent died.

For the most part I can't complain about my parents. Overall, they
did their best for both me and my brother. We never wanted for anything
while growing up. We weren't the richest people on the street, but we
were not the poorest either. We were raised with good morals and values,
we respected neighbors and always were ready to help anyone needing it.

I hope one day my boys will be able to say as much about Vicki and
me. If they do, I couldn't think of a better honor.

Respect for elders and each other in general has seemed to not have
the same priority in our society today as it once did.

Giving honor and respect to those who have taken care of us and
supported us throughout our lives should be a "given." Unfortunately
today that is not the case.

Including myself let me say without a doubt there has never been a
parent who hasn't "messed up" in some way raising their children and
I can guarantee that all future parents will do the same. So if you think

your childhood should have been one bed of roses you are fooling yourself and if you think you will be the perfect parent you're lying to yourself.

Paying honor to your parents shows your own character development. By honoring your parents, you are honoring yourself. You are demonstrating your own values and moral compass. You also are following the Christian principles of Exodus 20:12: "Honor your father and your mother."

CHAPTER 3

Leviticus *"Hate"*

"Thou shalt not hate thy brother in thine heart: thou shalt in any wise rebuke thy neighbor and not suffer sin upon him." Leviticus 19:17

Hate is in my opinion the dirtiest four-letter word. It represents everything that is wrong in the world. It destroys individuals, relationships, marriages, families, and careers. Hate is the cancer of the soul.

When we spend our energy on revenge, deception or even gossip we are practicing forms of hate.

Hate is an obsession. The longer a person hates the more intense the hate becomes. But the intensity of hate works twice as damaging on the one doing the hating. It burns the mind, causes blood pressure to soar and can cause stroke or worse. It can cause a person to even turn on those loved most.

The idea of not having your brother or neighbor is both spiritually and physically right.

Hate has played such a huge role in our world's development. Wars, crimes, even divorces have all been motivated by hate.

Let me me very clear: hate is a motivator. Hate is an extremely powerful motivator. It leaves much damage in its path some of which is non repairable.

Hate is also inherent. If you look at many of the longest running conflicts throughout the world, many from biblical times, you notice that those conflicts are still active because they have become generational.

The hate instilled by the forefathers continues through their descendants to this day, I.e. Mideast, Asia, Africa. Many fighting in those type of conflicts was born into them and nurtured by the hate of their ancestors.

Love thy brother and thy neighbor. Let love be the therapy that dissolves hate.

CHAPTER 4

Numbers *"Lying"*

"If a man vow a vow unto the Lord, or swear an oath to bind his soul with a bond he shall not break his word, he shall do according to all that proceedeth out of his mouth." Numbers 30:2

I SUPPOSE THE ONE PERSONALITY CHARACTERISTIC I dislike most is lying. The world unfortunately is composed of many who lie. I look at lying the same way I feel about cheating and taking short-cuts.

Lying, not keeping your word: both are representative of not being able to be trusted.

I try with all my heart to keep every obligation I make to anyone. That is not to say that I have always been successful. There are always going to be situations that come up in our lives where we are prevented from keeping our word.

When I am unable to do something, I have promised I immediately notify whoever I have obligated myself to and apologize and offer to reschedule. It shows two important points: (1) I respect the person I made the obligation to and (2) it shows my word can be trusted.

When it comes to making promises to the Lord, the chances are good that many of us, usually in times of hardship or trouble, do what I call "bargaining" with God. It's the old, "I promise I'll do this for you if you will just do that for me," routine.

How many times have people made you that promise and then once you do whatever they wanted you to do they suddenly have a loss of memory on what they promised.

Another point about promises they are most often first made by the person wanting something. Rarely does someone who doesn't want anything initiate a promise. And guess who is the one to break promises: in most cases the person who wanted something to begin with.

Finally let me say one thought regarding breaking promises to God: Don't! If you find yourself struggling to keep a promise that's very likely because Satan is encouraging, you to break it for that's what he wants. My advice is when you are struggling with keeping your promise to God, talk to Him about it. He already knows your being tested anyway so in reality it's no big secret. God never gets annoyed when someone comes to Him for guidance but that's not how He feels when a promise to Him is broken.

CHAPTER 5

Deuteronomy *"Respect"*

"'Cursed is he who dishonors his father or mother; and all the people shall say Amen.'" Deuteronomy 27:16

I F YOU LOOK AT THE word 'respect,' one of the most critical areas of life where it should be applied is with parents.

Honoring our parents has always been to me a "given." I'm not naive enough to believe every parent deserves respect. Our news media daily has horrid stories of violent, physical, and emotional abuse some parents place on their children.

Any individual who has been abused is going to be very reluctant to respect and honor someone who has hurt them particularly deliberately, and certainly when it is a parent.

History is full of stories about parental abuse. Children beaten, molested, killed by their parents.

Unfortunately, as with many other situations in life, the bad gets more attention than the good. There are many good parents who feed, clothe, educate and most importantly, love their children.

Many parents sit up nights helping their kids do homework, spend countless hours at ballparks, football games and work overtime or even two jobs to pay for school clothes and college tuition, to spend time impressing on them the importance of faith and the love of God.

The good parents instill self-respect, integrity and a quality value system that hopefully withstand the child's lifetime.

A child raised well will honor the parent in the best possible way: the parent will live within the child. The greatest honor, the greatest show of respect a parent can ever hope for by their child is to have that child to reflect the life that raised it.

CHAPTER 6

Joshua *"You're Not Alone"*

"....Be strong and of a good courage; neither thou be dismayed: for the Lord, thy God is with thee whithersoever thou guest." Joshua 1;9

I N TODAY'S WORLD BEING ALONE is in a word, "scary." We all face many challenges going through life. And there is something horrible about the idea of facing life alone. Life presents so many obstacles that facing them alone can be more than overwhelming.

Being fearless in life should not be confused with being reckless. Facing challenges, no matter how intense, must be done with caution and strategy.

I've always thought of being brave as facing challenges, not backing down, and being self-assured and prepared.

Being brave, being fearless and knowing you're not alone in life are all qualities of a devout Christian.

Knowing that God is always present in our lives is an assurance of peace, protection and a partnership with one we know can always be trusted, depended upon and who loves us.

CHAPTER 7

Judges *"Honor"*

"Now therefore if ye have done truly and sincerely in that ye have made Abimelech king, and if ye have dealt well with Jerubbaal and his house and have done unto him according to the deserving of his hands.". *Judges 9:16*

IN JUDGES 9:16, THE CENTRAL theme involves honor, good faith, and fairness. In a lot of my lectures and writings I refer to my parents. Now I do so again as I remember them always telling my brother Jerry and me to always treat people the way you would want them to treat you.

The opposite of honor is disrespect. There is no one who wants to be disrespected. And yet disrespect seems to follow all of us from childhood to the grave.

As children we all faced some type of bullying; we all faced some types of humiliation. Granted much of this disrespect wasn't as severe as many of the stories we currently hear about bullying, but the results still left scars and still hurts as much today as when it happened.

Disrespect comes in many other forms as well. In relationships, employment, even in how we worship. Our world has become so complex and due to social media and information circulating almost instantly, many times inaccurately, disrespect of our fellow man is rampant in our society. Many of us today believe the first "thing" we hear with no desire to consider it isn't true. The reality is we not only disrespect others, but we are disrespecting our own intelligence.

Everyone likes to be treated truthfully and in good faith. There is a saying, "a man's word is his bond."

Does it bother you when someone tells you they are going to do something for you and then it never happens? That's dealing in bad faith. I do believe there are times when circumstances can keep certain events from happening but dealing in bad faith is a continuous and habitual characteristic that gives the individual a reputation that they never seem to shake.

I've always tried to be fair to people. I once heard on a television show, "the only thing about fair is it comes once a year." Shamefully there is more truth to that statement than not.

Our society today seems to have evolved into a culture of "short-cuts." We want to get to the prize without paying the price. Skipping steps, stepping on other people, changing the rules when they don't suit us, whatever it takes to get where we want to go as quick and easy as possible. It's true in business, sports, government and our personal lives: getting there isn't half the fun, getting there is every man for himself.

Earning something is not "a fair day's wage for a fair day's work," anymore in so many of our lives. We have put fairness on a low priority and it's very evident in our society today.

Honor, good faith, and fairness. Written so long ago in Judges 9:16 is still so important today in creating positive and productive lifestyles.

CHAPTER 8

Ruth *"Never Being Alone"*

"…..for whither thou goest, I will go; and where thou lodgest, I will lodge: thy people shall be my people, and my God, my God…." Ruth 1:16

THERE IS A GOOD FEELING about knowing you are not alone, particularly in difficult times. There is even a better feeling knowing you will never be alone in times of trouble.

Every Christian will no doubt have his or her own personal reasons for loving God. If we all made a list of the top ten reasons, we are happy Christ is in our lives, we most likely all would include "never being alone" as one.

Loneliness is a terrible ordeal for anyone to suffer. Yet each year millions of people in the United States suffer from being alone.

Those who are homeless, widow or widower, those abandoned and those just running from their troubles spend countless days, nights, months and even years by themselves. In bad weather months there are many found frozen to death under bridges, in back alleys and in abandoned houses.

Unfortunately for most of these people they never realize the answer to their loneliness is one prayer away. God wants to be with us. Both in the good times and the bad God will be there for us. All we must do is invite him into our life.

CHAPTER 9

1 Samuel *"The Heart"*

"But the Lord said unto Samuel, look not on his countenance,
or on the height of his stature; because I have refused him: for
the Lord seeth not as man seeth; for man looketh on the outward
appearance, but the Lord looketh on the heart." 1 Samuel 16:7

W HAT DO YOU LOOK FOR in a person or are you looking for anything in particular?

Most of us probably aren't looking for anything initially when we first meet someone.

When I was teaching interviewing classes for college seniors getting ready to enter the job market, I always told them first impressions are critical in job interviews. That shouldn't necessarily be but to many employers how you first present yourself is more important than your qualifications.

Businesses always want a bubbly, well-dressed individual as the receptionist to give an initial positive impression on customers as it reflects the company's personality.

These are all external characteristics. They are what we notice about others. Human beings look at the physical.

God looks at the heart. God looks at the inner person. God doesn't care how handsome, beautiful, or muscular you are. He sees the real you and me. He sees our inner self.

God knows the heart not only controls the body physically but also emotionally and internally. He knows the heart controls the inner self, the behavior, attitude, and values.

Choosing your friends based on what you observe from their hearts is the only way to find true friendship.

CHAPTER 10

2 Samuel *"Walk with Us"*

"God is my strength and power: and he maketh
my way perfect." 2 Samuel 22:33

HOW COULD ANY INDIVIDUAL NOT be motivated to move forward in life knowing God is the center of his or her strength and power?

Life's pathways are often difficult and dangerous. Even though it may look otherwise at times few if any of us have had a completely casual stroll through life.

There's no question life has many dark valleys and there is nothing that says life is fair. When we travel down life's roads of uncertainty it is comforting to know the most powerful force ever is with us protecting us.

God does indeed arm us with strength and courage and paves our way through life if we accept him and believe in him.

He is indeed our strength and power and he can and will make our path safe. We just must ask him to walk that walk with us.

CHAPTER II

1 Kings *"Obedience"*

*"And if you walk in obedience to me and keep my decrees and commands
as David your father did, I will give you a long life." 1 Kings 3:14*

FOLLOWING THE LAW AND TREATING people with respect are good ways
to live your life.

There are always consequences following any action. Some may call
them reactions.

I have found that in most cases people like being treated well and
respected. Further I have found those same people respond in like manner.

Obedience is a word we don't hear much anymore. Obedience simply
means to obey or comply. Who in your life are you obedient to? Many
of us probably were first obedient to our parents. Then possibly our
teachers. But as we grow up, we find ourselves less inclined to be obedient
to anyone.

Society today, although in desperate need of structure and discipline,
rejects any form of control. Today we seem to have lost our sense of
respect and consideration for others. Destruction of others property,
intimidation, threats, and outright disregard for other people's feelings
are prominent.

In our society's current state the attitude is 'the rule hasn't been made
that can't be broken.' Our values system has certainly decayed in recent

years. Our disrespect for authority has almost been glorified in many media outlets.

Faith and belief are most likely the two strongest weapons we as Christians have in the battle to keep values and sense of responsibility prominent in our lives as well as an obedience to law and respect.

CHAPTER 12

2 Kings *"Faith and Belief"*

"...I have heard your prayer; I have seen your tears;
surely I will heal you." 2 Kings 20:5

OVER MY YEARS IN COUNSELING one fact I think all clients have in common is that they at one time or another shed tears and suffered pain in some form.

Not that this is a shocking statement because I feel safe in saying there isn't one of us living today that has not had the same experiences.

For sure depression many times results in emotional pain and can lead to physical pain in some instances.

So, what do we do and how do we cope with pain, suffering and depression? Psychologists and psychiatrists have been working on that problem for years.

As Christians although we do go to various counselors and doctors, we also go to God. Prayer is a Christian's strongest medicine against pain.

So, is pain and tears how God let's our bodies react to bad things? When God sees the tears, He not only already knows why He knows how and when it will stop.

He can stop the tears and stop the pain. He can make it all better, however, He wants to be sure we know what's going on.

He also wants to know we have faith and belief in Him. Asking for help from God is proof of our realization that He is real, caring, loving and compassionate. He wants you to know that when He believes the time is right, He will heal you.

CHAPTER 13

1 Chronicles *"Trust"*

"....for they called to God in the battle and he was intreated of them because they put their trust in Him." 1 Chronicles. 5:20

T RUST MIGHT BE THE MOST important quality a person could have. Trust could be defined as a "bond" between two or more parties but also it could be a "bond" between the individual and the soul.

Do you trust your instincts? Some people say they trust their "gut" feeling about things regardless of physical evidence. Is it a feeling resulting from past experiences, is it a judgement call based more on what you know than what you don't know?

It's interesting that when a newborn baby comes into the world there seems to be a "built-in" trust between the child and the mother instantly. The child's cries are softened, its fears lessened, and its complete attention immediately focused on the mother's touch or mere presence.

We often see trust between animals and humans. For example, most of us have had a pet dog that no matter how dangerous a situation you are in will rush to your side and place itself in danger to protect you. It's because a trusting bond has been developed. The dog knows you will love and take care of it under any circumstance and it feels the same for you.

So why wouldn't God be there for you? The answer is: He will be. If you trust and believe in Him, then He will be there to guide your life.

When you have asked God to come into your life, when you repent for your sins, you will be forgiven, and that forgiveness shows the trust and love God has for you. He will answer your prayers because you have trusted in Him.

CHAPTER 14

2 Chronicles *"Mercy"*

"...for He is good: for His mercy endureth forever". 2 Chronicles.

WHEN YOU TALK ABOUT MOTIVATION the statement in 2 Chronicles "...for He is good: for His mercy endured forever," it's very possible that could be the best motivational statement ever made.

There are a couple of points I think are important about mercy.

First, we need to remember that as God bestows His mercy so should we be willing to show mercy for others.

Helping others who are in need: people who are hurting and suffering whether we know them or not. And do you find it hard to show mercy to those who have hurt you or your family?

Second, mercy does not include holding vendettas and grudges forever. To truly be merciful there must be a element of forgiveness as well. Showing mercy also involves forgiveness.

Forgiveness and mercy bestowed on not only those in need but those who have caused you harm or distress is indeed mercy from your heart.

As "His mercy endured forever" so should our mercy be there for others and in reality for the betterment of our souls.

CHAPTER 15

Ezra *"Taking Charge"*

"Rise up, take charge and do it." Ezra 10:4

S OMETHING I HAVE NEVER BEEN fond of is the sayings, "let's wait and see what happens," along with, "worry about tomorrow, tomorrow." Then there is another popular but pathetic comment: "Somebody needs to do something."

God gave all of us a free will. With it He included responsibility. He expects us to be responsible for the decisions we make both good and bad.

Depending on others to take the initiative for something that could benefit you or your family rather than stepping up to the plate and doing it yourself is both insulting to yourself and deliberately refusing to use the abilities God has given you.

There is absolutely nothing wrong with not knowing how to do certain things. I can vouch for not knowing about a multitude of different things. However, God gives all of us the ability to learn. To some learning is easier than it is for others. That's part of the uniqueness God also gave each of us. So even though we may not know how to take charge and deal with some events we still can find ways to move forward that will get us through the current troubling situation.

As the Bible is full of stories with people rising up and taking charge in different situations so should we rise up and take charge in our own lives.

CHAPTER 16

Nehemiah *"Success"*

"The God of heaven, he will prosper us; therefore, we His
servants will arise and build." Nehemiah 2:20

I HAVE HAD THE OPPORTUNITY TO sit in many great seminars regarding success both personal and professional.

Some of the finest motivational speakers in the world have lectures on acquiring a positive attitude, as well as a successful life and career.

The best speakers I have ever listened to regarding success always referred to a strong Christian philosophy and credit God for making the success a reality.

There are many theories and ideas on how to become successful whether from a business standpoint or in individual personality development.

Of those success formulas expounded by authors, psychologists, college professors, and professional development organizations, all encourage certain intrinsic attributes that directly or indirectly are of Christian origin.

There are many ways to "understand" what a positive attitude or approach to life is but it requires and internal effort by the individual to make that attitude work and that effort comes from the grace of God.

At the conclusion of various sporting events it is not unusual to hear the winning athletes give credit to God during interviews rightfully realizing without His blessings there would have been no victory.

Additionally most if not all Christians regularly give credit to God for all their success and achievements whether for personal reasons, educational success or professional achievement.

It is true that the God of the heavens is the one who will grant us success.

CHAPTER 17

Esther *"Time"*

"Perhaps this is the moment for which you have been created." Esther 4:14

THERE WAS A POPULAR STATEMENT used in several political ads a few years ago that said, "this is our time."

If you look at history you can see how during certain events there were particular individuals that were in position to deal with that specific situation.

For example, it was President Roosevelt who was in the White House as the nation faced the Great Depression, Dwight Eisenhower who led us through World War II, George W. Bush who was in charge during 9-1-1.

There are so many more examples of people who were in the right place at the right time. But was it the "right" time or should we say was it when God wanted them to be there?

You have most likely heard the phrase, "it's your destiny." There are many people who believe they were born to lead, even to rule. Entitlement is probably the word.

I truly believe God has a purpose for each of us in life and a "time" for us to make that purpose work for His glory. For many of us that purpose and time may come relatively early in life while for others it may come towards the end of our lives or even midway through our journeys on earth. And there most likely are some who may even go through their entire lives, fulfill their purpose and never ever realized it.

So, it comes down to knowing not when you have a "time" or what your purpose will be in life but realizing that God has one for you. That's motivation.

CHAPTER 18

Job *"Light of Hope"*

*"And thou shalt be secure, because there is hope...Also thou shalt
lay down and none shall make thee afraid." Job 11: 18, 19*

HOPE IS A WORD WE hear a lot but do we really know what hope is? Hope is the stimulus that keeps people going in the absolute worst and most desperate of times.

It is the hope that things will get better and things will improve that lets us keep our sanity and maintain our responsibilities in the crisis situations of life.

Hope gives us the opportunity to improve our lives. Hope is the motivational tool that pushes us when nothing else will.

Hope stimulates courage. The beautiful thing about hope is that God gives us hope to make changes in areas of our lives where we might feel helpless.

Hope also comes from faith. In order to have hope you first must have faith. God does indeed give us hope but we must believe in Him. God gives us the light of hope to move into dark areas of our lives and to have the courage to make changes needed for a prosperous and successful life.

Having hope will give you courage, having hope will give you peace, having hope means you have faith and having faith means you have God.

CHAPTER 19

Psalms *"Blessed is he that considers the poor"*

*"Blessed is he that considereth the poor; the Lord will
deliver him in time of trouble." Psalm 41*

I WILL ALWAYS REMEMBER COUNTRY-WESTERN SINGER Johnny Cash saying on many of his television shows, "God must have loved poor people because he sure made a lot of them."

Normally when we think of poor people, we think of folks who live in run-down neighborhoods, not having much food or money, no employment and basically living day to day.

People however are poor in many other ways and sometimes not even their closest friends or even family members ever realize it.

From a psychological standpoint it can be said many people are in poor emotional health. They are either suffering from chronic depression or acute periods of low self-esteem, paranoia, and other personality disorders.

From a physical standpoint it can be said many people suffer poor health from various injuries, as well as inherited and contacted diseases.

Among several definitions given, Webster's II dictionary defines "poor "as "lacking in mental or moral quality." So, we can include poor judgment and poor decision making in life.

What I am trying to point out is that there are many ways to help and assist the poor. Sometimes it's not only with money or food, sometimes it's with counsel or just friendship. Helping the poor can be done in so many ways but the result is similar: It all comes down to being willing to help those in need.

Regardless of the need, helping your fellow man or woman in need is in fact helping the poor. We are all poor in one way or another at one time or another.

Motivationally, this quote fits very well: "Blessed is the one who considers the poor! In the day of trouble, the Lord delivers him."

CHAPTER 20

Proverbs *"Anxiety"*

"Anxiety weighs down the heart, but a kind word
cheers it up." Proverbs 12:25. NIV

D ID YOU EVER WONDER WHY we let anxiety overtake our daily lives? And what is so important in our lives that makes our emotions cause us physical problems?

After years of working with athletes, students, business owners, teachers and other blue collar and white collar workers I have realized one of the key denominators all of us have in common with regard to causing anxiety is: we are all searching.

We are all searching in life for a kind word, a pat on the back, a "atta-boy." Our egos demand that we continually search for approval in life and if we don't get it we can't rest.

There are rewards for good work and good deeds. Money is the obvious sign of approval for most. How much money made is a stamp of approval for work. The big home, new car and where you vacation all serve as "pats on the back" for our egos. They also serve as a picture to our neighbors, family and friends of "how well" we are doing.

So if you have the financial reward, even the successful children going to the best colleges, the great public reputation, why the anxiety?

Anxiety comes from confusion in the heart. The pulling of emotional strings that stretch from one way of thinking to another. Anxiety comes from thinking you want to do something one way while your subconscious tells you to do it another.

Many times, there is no right or wrong choice you might make. It's the anticipation that one decision may be the wrong one that causes you the sleepless nights, not thinking clearly and second-guessing yourself.

There are two types of anxiety: group anxiety and individual anxiety. With group anxiety there's normally a project, work, family, or class project where others share in the stress over the same situation.

Then there is individual anxiety. This is where most of us suffer. We are out there all alone. If the outcome is positive, it's all fantastic but if the outcome is bad, we know we take all the blame.

It's the individual anxiety we must find a way to deal with. This type of anxiety puts grey hair, high blood pressure, heart disease and worse in our lives. What we need is reassurance: not just the knowledge but the belief that things will be ok.

Many of us turn to God in extreme times of anxiety for that "well-done," or "atta-boy." Others find peace in writing, exercise, or meditation.

Personally, I believe most anxiety is the result of not being satisfied with ourselves; not the issue at hand but an unhappiness or insecurity within us about us. How we deal with ourselves both on the inside and outside is what I believe we are really searching for. We are looking for that kind word about us to come from us.

CHAPTER 21

Ecclesiastes *"Anger"*

"Be not quick in your spirit to become angry, for anger
lodges in the heart of fools." Ecclesiastes 7:9

ANGER IS CERTAINLY A MOTIVATOR. There isn't any of us who hasn't experienced anger and there isn't any of us who won't experience anger again.

Anger has led good people to do some very bad things. Anger has turned friend against friend, spouse against spouse, child against parent and even country against country.

Uncontrolled anger may very well be the most destructive and unforgiving motivator known. It's power and intensity are difficult if not impossible to gage.

So the question becomes: how do we let this extreme motivator be turned from ruthless to invaluable?

One of the first points to consider is anger has no compass: it is wild, reckless and without guidance. You on the other hand can decide how important it is to be angry, for how long, and to what intensity. If you control those points you control anger.

One other point about anger. It can be fatal. It not only can lead you to physically harming others, but it can cause you to harm yourself. Anger causes stress, high blood pressure, heart disease, stroke, not to mention emotional distress and nervous breakdowns.

Once anger lodges in your heart and obsession with all that goes with it takes over your ever-waking moment you become paralyzed with the inability to be rational, creative or productive.

Controlling anger and manipulating it to make your life productive and not destructive is the key to keeping it from your heart and soul. Make anger a positive motivator.

CHAPTER 22

Song of Solomon *"Love"*

*"Many waters cannot quench love, neither can the floods drown
it; if a man would give all the substance of his house for love
it would be utterly contemned" Song of Solomon. 8:7*

L OVE MAY VERY WELL BE the most powerful word in the English language. The element of love is present in so many situations and can motivate when no other form of motivation seems effective.

There has been much written about the intensity of a mother's love. It's the bond that ties child to mother emotionally if both live.

Love is the bond that ties men and women together in marriage and then wraps itself around their children and produces the family structure.

The world has always been fascinated by the concept of love. Passion, intimacy and loyalty are all recalled when we hear the word "love. "Compassion and affection are automatically thought of In our culture when discussing love.

Another Bible verse from Corinthians states, "These three things continue forever, Faith, Hope and Love and the greatest of these is Love." Corinthians 13:13.

I do believe the greatest love however was God's love for mankind that was so great He let His own son die so we might live. What better act to motivate all of us to live a good and productive life?

CHAPTER 23

Isaiah *"Arise and Shine"*

"Arise, shine; for thy light is come; and the glory of
the Lord is risen upon thee." Isaiah 60:01

THE DARKEST USUALLY COMES BEFORE we see the light.
With the Covet 19 pandemic it surely seems we have been definitely extending the darkness.

There has been so much confusion and uncertainty in life throughout this pandemic and although a vaccine may be on the horizon it is only for the virus not for the feelings of hopelessness and depression that many of us are suffering.

Darkness has beset our nation in so many ways. The terrorist attack of 9-1-1 left the country shocked and terrified. The Boston marathon bombing horrified us and the Columbine shootings stunned our nation.

The American family unit has been under extreme stress in recent times as our values system has come under attack more intensely than ever before. Families have never experienced the division from within that now occurs. Single-parent families or children being raised by grandparents have become more of a norm today whether because of either need or choice.

Adding to the dark times are the social problems of drug abuse, violent crime, child abuse and the high rate of homeless that live on the nations streets and alleys.

But as the verse in Isaiah 60:01 states, "Arise, shine; for thy light is come; and the glory of the Lord is risen upon thee." We can take solace in and be motivated by the belief that God has brought light to our world. These problems and many more similar will be solved as the light of the Lord shines upon us. All we must do is open our eyes.

CHAPTER 24

Jeremiah *"For a Reason"*

"You are here for a reason." Jeremiah 28:11

There isn't any of us, if we were being totally honest, that has not at one time, or another wondered what reason God has for our lives.

I can tell you from personal experience I have thought about that many times over the years and still do.

What I've found is that although I do believe God has a plan for all of us He's not going to reveal it until He's good and ready.

I've been blessed with some pretty good jobs over my career: mental health care, education, coaching, business, politics, counseling, and now being an author. I can tell you through all of that I really am not sure why He chose me to do those things.

There certainly are some constants: all involved working with people, providing some type of assistance, public service. As a result I have come to feel He believes I evidently am good at helping others.

Now that's just my assumption but as long as he lets me continue through life I believe He will continue to point me in certain directions whether I think I am capable of doing it or not and I will go down those avenues of life trying to give it my best shot.

Part of being a Christian is believing God has a plan; not just a individual plan for each of us but an overall plan for all of us together. Believing that one day a grand plan will be revealed is the motivation that all of us of faith wait on.

CHAPTER 25

Lamentations *"Mistakes"*

"God's mercy is greater than any of your mistakes,". Lamentations 3:22-23

H ERE'S A FACT THAT A surprisingly high number of people seem to not believe: No living human being has not made mistakes and the same is true for every dead human.

Mistakes are a part of living. None of us were born to not "mess" something up every now and then. Some of us mess up more than others but we're all guilty and will be if we live.

What matters about mistakes is not so much that we make them but it's what we learn from them.

Unfortunately, today we have a very critical attitude toward each other. We all know people who, while never doing anything productive themselves, immediately pounce on someone who makes a mistake while trying to be successful. What really compounds the problem is that many people who make honest mistakes and then get openly criticized by others will give up on trying again.

It's safe to say no one starts out their day deliberately wanting to mess something up No one begins the day deliberately trying to cause chaos and havoc. Mistakes are just that: mistakes.

Learning from mistakes is the most common way to learn. In my days as a teacher I had to learn through trial and error how to reach different students. All kids are different, and I made plenty of mistakes trying to teach them.

The same thing is true in counseling. I've made plenty of mistakes trying different methods and ideas to understand where each client is coming from with their problems and issues.

I've come to believe that anyone who says they've never made a mistake is either a liar or dead. Those who deny their mistakes are making a mistake. And to deny rather than learn from them is just ignorance.

God does indeed forgive mistakes. He knows we are humans. He created us. God's mercy is indeed greater than any of our mistakes.

CHAPTER 26

Ezekiel *"Attitude"*

"A new heart also will I give you, and a new spirit
will I put within you....". Ezekiel 36:26

A ttitude is most likely to be one of the first characteristics of someone's personality that you notice.

I think it is fair to say that attitude is a mirror of the individual.

One of the early important decisions any new business must make is the attitude it displays to the public. Is the new company going to be one which involves its employees in community events; is it going to be a community leader in various causes of concern to the public? Or will the company choose to stay "under the radar," carry out its day-to-day activities and stay virtually invisible?

I've always maintained that people who work reception areas are the most important employees in any company. Why? They are the first people met by the public on any given business day. The attitude these folks have on that initial meeting is the first impression given of the company. Positive first impressions are often crucial in all relationships, personal and business.

We need also to look at our individual attitudes. God gives each of us the opportunity to develop our personalities as we go through life.

Personality development is nurtured by environment. Where we live, work and the friends we keep are all factors in our personality.

You have heard the phrase, "people change," and they do change.

Changes in environment do change attitudes. The attitude change is more specifically a change in heart.

People also change when they become people of faith. A new attitude, different priorities, a completely new approach to life. God does put a new spirit, a feeling of love and caring in us which changes negative feelings and makes life appear more worthwhile and exciting.

CHAPTER 27

Daniel *"Fear"*

*"...O man, greatly beloved, fear not: peace be unto
thee, be strong, yea be strong..." Daniel 10:19*

F EAR IS A UGLY FOUR-LETTER word. It is a word that is used to manipulate
and to scare. It is used to cause terror, hate, and can force people to
even kill.

People have done so many dramatic things over the years out of
fear. There are several reactions to fear, among them, stopping what you
are doing, running away from something or someone and wanting to
physically fight.

I do think fear has some good uses. It is important to fear dangerous
situations: uncontrolled fires, dangerous chemicals, contagious diseases,
wild animals. Fear does serve in those and similar situations to protect
us from imminent harm.

Another point to make about fear: it keeps us in our comfort zone.
Human beings tend to become complacent or embedded in their comfort
zones. There is a fear of the unknown or of change. Change causes fear, a
fear of the unknown and of failing. Fear of change causes us to be unsure
of ourselves at times or taking on new challenges, a new job or even a
new relationship.

Finally fear handicaps our attempts to reach potential, to grow both
physically and emotionally. Success, both personally and professionally

is only going to happen by overcoming fear. Success with personal and professional growth are only possible by not succumbing to fear.

God is there to help us overcome our fears. He will give us courage and He will give us guidance. All we must do is ask Him.

CHAPTER 28

Hosea *"Bless the Merciful"*

"Say to your brothers, 'You are my people and to your
sisters, you have received mercy." Hosea 2:1 ESV

MERCY IS A COMPLICATED PROCESS for many people. Although in times of trouble most everyone is ready to accept mercy it's not something everyone is always ready to give.

In general most people interpret mercy to mean helping people who are hurting or in some form of distress and that includes people who may have at one time or another caused you problems.

I think another point to make about mercy is it shouldn't be confused with forgiveness. It's important to forgive and not be ate up with hate and revenge but having mercy on someone that has harmed you in some way, although being a step toward forgiveness, is not the same.

It's also important to point out that mercy and forgiveness are neither the same as forgetting. In truth many can forgive and even administer mercy but forgetting is many times much harder.

There are certainly many cases where our faith can be severely tested and the internal pressures for not forgiving or having any form of mercy on someone for a hideous or despicable act is intense.

In today's world values seem to either be changing daily or just don't exist. People are faced with challenges different than any the world has seen in generations. It is time to remember "God blesses those who are merciful, for they shall be shown mercy" (Matthew 5:7 NLT).

CHAPTER 29

Joel *"Be Good and Rejoice"*

*"Fear not, O land; be glad and rejoice for the
Lord will do great things." Joel 2:21*

As THIS PANDEMIC CONTINUES THROUGHOUT not only our country but the world, never has any event in recent history caused more personal reflection.

Fear of the unknown is normal and something we all experience at various points in our lives: As children on the first day of school; that first dentist appointment; buying your first house, etc.

In today's world or as it is being called, "the new normal," uncertainty and the anticipation of the unknown are becoming a part of our lifestyle.

So how do we cope with this new era of change? Who and what do we look to?

First I think it's important to remember something President Franklin Roosevelt said when taking office during the depression. His famous saying, "We have nothing to fear but fear itself."

We can and will find a vaccine and eventual cure for COVID. What we must do is not succumb to the fear and let it guide our lives. Human beings have proven over and over they are very resourceful. Positive thinking, following health guidelines and using common sense can go a long way in putting fear out of the equation.

Most importantly for us of faith is taking solace in God's word in Joel 2:21, "Fear not, O land; be glad and rejoice: for the Lord will do great things."

CHAPTER 30

Amos *"Seek Good"*

"Seek good and not evil, that ye may live and so the Lord, the God of hosts, shall be with you as ye have spoken". Amos 5:15

T HERE REALLY ISN'T A LOT of discussion today about good and evil. Less often do we hear much conversation about the virtues of being good or the repercussions of evil.

Society today doesn't appear to differentiate between right and wrong. Instead right or wrong are looked at as options.

Somewhere our generation has lost track of priorities. I recently read a quote attributed to President Theodore Roosevelt: "When you educate a man in mind and not in morals, you educate a menace to society." Today we have let educational theory override both common sense and responsibility.

Never in our history has a culture compromised it's values and principles as has been occurring in recent times.

There is no question people are confused. There is so much misinformation on social media and the internet; instead of looking for the right answers it's much easier to find an answer you want.

It is also important to remember God has given us the ability of free choice. But as we give our children free choice in certain areas as they grow, God has given us free choices as we grow and as we have consequences for our children's choices so does God have consequences for the choices we make.

Many today place convenience and pleasure over right and wrong. Responsibility appears to just get in our way. Seeking good over evil should be a way of life and yet to many it's only a distant thought.

CHAPTER 31

Obadiah *"Every Action has a Reaction"*

*"For the day of the Lord is near upon the heathen: as thou
hast done, it shall be done unto thee...". Obadiah 1:15*

W<small>E HEAR A LOT THESE</small> days about something called karma.
Essentially it means, "whatever goes around comes around."

There's no doubt that in life there are mean and cruel people who
hurt good people. Innocent people are hurt and even killed for no reason.

In recent months we have seen towns burned, senseless shootings
with young children playing in their front yards shot to death by drive-by
shootings. Innocent people have been hurt and killed. Senseless violence
has been the norm while common sense and reason are thrown away.

What's even more unbelievable is all of this is happening right here
in our own backyards. So, the question becomes, why?

Is much of the violence and unrest the result of us ignoring the very
principles which our country was founded? Have we forgot the sacrifice
and dedication it took our forefathers to build the foundation for which
we now live?

Earl Nightingale, a one-time nationally syndicated radio personality
and author said in his book, "The Strangest Secret," "Your returns in life
must be in direct proportion to what you give."

'That statement by Nightingale rings so very true. When we put
out effort whether to achieve good or bad, we will receive equivalent
to that effort. The harder you work at a task the closer you will come to

achieving it. The more people you help in life the more people will likely help you. But remember the more people you try to hurt in life the more people who are going to try hurting you when they get the chance.

The same principles apply in how we live. If we choose to live a life of good morals and values, we will receive the positive consequences that come with it. If we choose to live a life of corruption, lying and manipulation then our lives will be filled with those same negative features.

I have always believed that for every action there is a reaction. Could it be as is in Obadiah 1:15 "...as thou hast done, it shall be done unto thee,"?

CHAPTER 32

Jonah *"Keeping Vows"*

"But I will sacrifice unto thee with the voice of thanksgiving;
I will pay that that I have vowed....". Jonah 2:9

TODAY MOST OF US ARE immediately reminded when a bill payment is due. Either a phone call, mailed statement or both are sent to your home.

Paying debts either financially or in other ways has been a part of life for years. Most of us know that every "payday," one of the first things we do is set aside enough money to pay the mortgage, utility bills and any other debt we owe, most monthly.

There are other types of debt that many times we don't prioritize, however. For example, do we return good deeds to those who have done something good for us?

Do you repay emotional debts? Do you try to be there in times of crisis and pain for those that were there for you under the same circumstances?

And what about parents? The very people who brought you into the world, raised you, educated you and gave you the opportunity for a successful life. Is there really any way to repay that debt?

In his book, '7 Laws of Love,' David Willis says, "When we show kindness to those who will repay us, it's called 'networking;' when we show kindness with no thought of repayment it is called love."

There is no question some debts need to be repaid in kind. Love and appreciation are also repayment. Keep in mind your integrity is on the line when you owe any debt. Be sure the vow you make is a vow you keep.

CHAPTER 33

Nahum *"Trust"*

*"The Lord is good, a strong hold in the day of trouble; and
He knoweth them that trust in Him." Nahum 1:7*

T RUST CONTINUES TO BE THE most important trait in a human being's
life. Trust is the cement that holds together marriages, friendships,
family structures and business deals.

It's interesting to look at how trust is not only the common bond
for human interaction but for even animals. Pets develop bonds of trust
with humans and many will fight to the death defending their owners.
Racehorses develop bonds of trust with certain jockeys; animal trainers
must have bonds of trust with whatever animals in their charge. Trust is
the key to any success and with most species.

Trust although possibly the strongest bonding force is also the most
difficult to restore when broken. Apologies, making amends, regret, all
cannot rebuild the bond trust once held tightly.

Remember that true love and trust go together. It's very difficult to
love someone you don't trust. There's no doubt that many marriages built
on love and little or no trust don't survive long.

When people don't trust you it denies opportunity to reach full
potential. Trust is key when helping others. You perform better for
anyone when being trusted as it shows their confidence in you, your
skills and abilities.

It's certain that truth is the cornerstone of trust. Without truth, trust can only be tainted. The reward for trust is love, compassion and loyalty.

Finally, it is important to trust ourselves. Do we avoid unnecessary risks? Do we choose our friends and our relationships carefully? Do we watch our health, what we eat and drink? Self-trust is key in maturity. If you do not trust yourself how can it be expected for others to trust you?

CHAPTER 34

Micah *"Falling Down and Getting Up"*

"Though I fall, I will rise again." Micah 7:8

W E START FALLING AS A child starting to walk. In many ways we are just beginning because we then proceed to fall throughout the rest of our lives. Anyone who tells you that's not true is either in need of therapy or a profound liar.

Life is full of falling. It's not that important that you fall. What is important is whether you keep getting back up or not.

Human beings are not perfect; we are far from it. Being a Christian does not prevent us from making mistakes. Being a Christian does however give us the benefit of the greatest Counselor to help us straighten things out.

Giving up is the same as not getting back up. People who deserve so much admiration are those with terminal illness who fight to the very end. The unimaginable pain and suffering people with cancer, addiction, diabetes, and other chronic disease who keep fighting, some getting out of bed everyday are the real heroes, the fighters, the ones who do keep getting back up.

The same is true with those who grow up in poor underdeveloped parts of the world. These people fight to live every day. They do whatever jobs they need to do to feed their families and themselves. They get knocked down every day and keep getting back up.

Then we have the disabled, those born with birth defects, partial limbs, blind or with other hereditary issues. They get knocked down daily, but they get back up and live productive lives.

The world is full of so many stories of people knocked down, sometimes several times a day and giving up is never a consideration. Getting back up and moving on. Not worrying about getting knocked down, knowing they will get knocked down again but keep on keeping on.

CHAPTER 35

Habakkuk *"Impatience"*

*"If it seems slow, wait for it, it surely will come,
it will not delay." Habakkuk 2:3*

IMPATIENCE SEEMS MORE AND MORE to be the description of our culture today. Waiting is not looked at as a virtue but rather as a liability in our personal lives, business lives and even in our worship.

I am certainly guilty of wanting everything immediately when I was younger. I know I was one who didn't spend a lot of time worrying about detail. As I have gotten older, I have learned early avoidance leads to late term chaos many times.

Based on my own experiences I do understand the "wanting it now" philosophy. It's not fair to say impatience is only a characteristic of youth. Our culture today, young, and old, shares the adjective of impatience.

With the world economy on a fast track, foreign governments in turmoil, and a total confusion of moral values immediacy without regard for consequences is the prevailing attitude

In order for our society to have any chance of a productive future it must at least slow down, take inventory of where we are, and develop a positive path forward.

We must as a people, look at our situation, ask ourselves why mistrust, dissension and immorality continue to grow. We do need to be mindful that honesty in answers is key.

Waiting may not be appealing but slowing down and taking our time is prudent and responsible. Weighing consequences and remembering that every action has a reaction is critical. We need to remember that there is a lot to be said for, "if it seems slow, wait for it, it surely will come, it will not delay."

CHAPTER 36

Zephaniah *"Self-Control"*

"He is mighty to save, He will calm all your fears." Zephaniah 3:16, 3:17

I HAVE LONG BELIEVED THAT ONE of the strongest motivational words in the English language is "fear."

Fear motivates both positively and negatively. Good people sometimes do bad things and often the reason is fear. Fear of losing something or someone has been the motivating force for stealing, hurting others, even murder.

There are documented cases of murder being committed because of child custody, relationships, and even suicides all motivated because of fear of losing something or someone.

Fear can be a positive motivator: One arena is the health industry. Fear of illness is a motivator for check-ups, physical fitness gyms, mental health and addiction services and other health related issues.

The big question we have to answer involves how we face fear and how we manipulate it to our advantage rather than let it control us.

Fear isn't necessarily something to always be afraid of. We can use fear to motivate us. Doing what's right isn't always being afraid to make a mistake but rather realizing the benefits of doing the right thing.

Self-control is key in making fear motivate us in constructive ways. When you lose self-control, any fear will dominate and spread.

As it implies in 2 Timothy 1:7, "God didn't give us a spirit of fear, but of power, love and self-control."

CHAPTER 37

Haggai *"Thinking Things Through"*

"Don't get in a hurry and not think things through," a phrase my parents used to tell me on more than one occasion. I always have found that to be one of the best pieces of advice I've ever had".

WHEN I WAS IN HIGH school I remember being bombarded by mailings and telephone calls about attending different colleges, going in the military and countless other places wanting me and my classmates to spend the next several years of our lives; and they wanted commitments as early as possible before any serious thought could be given.

Many of the decisions made today, in government, business and personally are not well thought out. We make too many decisions with a "spur of the moment" attitude, never giving any thought to consequences.

Our society has become a "I want it now" culture. That attitude has been reinforced by the many social media websites where you can purchase virtually anything from food to new cars by typing in a few numbers. The availability of anything at the tip of your fingers makes "thinking about it" a faint thought.

We need to take heed in giving thought to our ways. Thinking about what we do before we do it and considering future consequences is a sign of maturity and characteristic of a positive and successful person.

CHAPTER 38

Zechariah *"Hope-Feeling of Trust with Anticipation"*

"Turn you to the strong hold, ye prisoners of hope..." Zechariah 9:12

THERE ARE SEVERAL REASONS I wanted to include the word "hope" in the title of this book.

I have always believed hope is the greatest motivational word in our language. Hope is something that I believe to be part of our initial makeup at birth and its strength develops with maturity.

There are so many examples of hope: People faced with death or imminent danger, photos of people waiting in soup lines during the depression, photos of Jews in the Nazi concentration camps, photos of children hospitalized for cancer, birth defects and abuse, photos of elderly people alone in nursing homes. In the eyes of most all these people you can tell there is a glimmer of hope, no matter how small, that things will get better.

Hope gives us the possibility something good will eventually happen and everything will get better. Hope is a feeling of trust with anticipation of a better future. Hope is an intangible that exists in all of us and motivates us in the worst of times.

CHAPTER 39

Malachi *"Peace"*

"My covenant was with him of life and peace; and I gave them to him....he walked with me in peace and equity..." Malachi 2:5;6

THE ONE GOAL THAT WE'VE heard about all our lives from politicians and world leaders which continues to be preached is the goal of peace.

Webster's Dictionary defines peace as freedom from quarrels and disagreement; harmonious relations.

It has been throughout history that quarrels and disagreements have been the least of the violence; war and destruction have dominated world events for centuries.

Although there appears to be a continual search for peace it's discovery has been anything but easy. Yes, there has been times when wars and conflicts have not been as active but those periods of time have only been short-lived.

With regard to today's culture, disagreements have dominated network television news. Protests and violent demonstrations have caused cities and businesses to be burned. Hate and confusion dominate our lives either indirectly through various media outlets or directly in our personal lives where many families struggle with unemployment, addiction, alcoholism, COVET, and other intense problems that erupt into family warfare.

Inner peace can only be when we come to grips with our lives, prioritize what it is we want and place total focus in that direction. Peace of mind must be our highest personal goal to have both a successful and productive life.

The New Testament

CHAPTER 1

Matthew *"Humility"*

"Truly I say to you unless you turn and become like children you will never enter the kingdom of heaven. Whoever humbles himself like this child is the greatest in the kingdom of heaven." Matthew 18:3-4

H UMILITY IS A VIRTUE THAT we don't seem to hear much about these days. In a world where the loudest voice usually gets the quickest response fewer people today practice being humble.

My brother and I were always taught to not "blow your own horn." Bragging about yourself in our family was looked at as arrogant and rude. Sports was the same way be a team player, don't be a "ball hog." I still believe being taught the benefits of being humble as a child helps develop you as a person.

Unfortunately, much of the world today can't wait to tell everyone how great they are. Politicians, athletes, business leaders and many other people can't wait to tell you why you need them, their service, or their products in your life.

Being humble today is difficult to say the least. When I used to do job interviews, I was stunned at how applicants would so blatantly tell me how great they were and why I needed them. Later I learned through friends that is how job applicants are trained and how to behave in interviews.

I've maintained for several years what I call the "All about me" syndrome has taken a major role in our culture. And I believe the lack of humility that we see among many today is a symptom of that syndrome.

We need to work toward bringing many values currently discarded back into our culture. Arrogance and selfishness have no place in a productive successful society.

So in regard to being humble, it's important to remember as it says in Matthew 18:3, "Verily I say unto you, Except ye be converted and become as little children, ye shall not enter into the kingdom of heaven."

CHAPTER 2

Mark *"Courage"*

*"And Jesus stood still and commanded him to be called and they called
saying: 'Take courage; Get up, the Lord is calling you.'" Mark 10:49*

W E'VE HEARD THE WORD "COURAGE," many times in our lives.
Courage is defined in Webster's dictionary as "the quality or state
of mind or spirit enabling one to face danger or hardship with confidence
or resolution."

Courage certainly comes in many sizes. When I was teaching the first
day of school for kids was a show of courage. I remember seeing many
preschool children coming in that first day with their parents and then
the look in their eyes when mom and dad left them in the classroom.
They were just preschool, but you could see the courage in their eyes as
for most it was the first time they were on their own.

Of course there are many other more serious and intense forms
of courage. Soldiers going off to war, people with terminal illnesses,
children with disabilities, the list can be long.

So it's fair to say that it's the courage we watch in others that motivates
us to greater heights, more success.

It is important to remember not to confuse courage with arrogance.
People who are arrogant only take actions to impress their own ego.
There is no attempt to motivate when being arrogant but rather to only
impress yourself.

Courage is a motivator. It motivates the individual and others. It takes courage to go back to school after many years to earn that diploma. It takes courage to start your own business. And it takes courage to admit you are wrong. Courage impresses and motivates just as God encourages and motivates us.

Can you be sure you motivate others through your displays of courage?

CHAPTER 3

Luke *"Authority"*

"Behold I have given you authority; to tread on serpants and scorpians, and over all the power of the enemy, and nothing shall hurt you." Luke 10:19

AUTHORITY IS A COMPLEX WORD. It can be applied to many aspects of life: relationships, parenting, business, etc.

Authority is in many ways synonymous with control, and like control, authority comes with responsibility. Just not responsibility for the task at hand being completed successfully but also in the proper ways to manage human beings.

Human behavior is probably as diverse today as it has ever been. Personalities are ever changing. Feelings get hurt easier, emotions show quicker and attitudes change at a rapid pace.

History shows us many forms of authoritarian abuse from kings and pharaohs to dictators and presidents. World events and the course of mankind have all been chartered one way or the other by authoritarian decisions both good and bad.

In the United States much authority is given to our government through the votes of the citizenry. Decisions on the economy, finance, health, and legislative actions are determined by assigned authority of the people.

Authority in business by leadership can make or break an entire industry. Companies have come and gone because those chosen to lead have abused or not taken seriously the responsibility required.

I believe the abuse or misuse of authority in personal relationships and in parenting has caused much heartache and suffering in families.

Authority must be accompanied with common sense and reason. Proper knowledge and appreciation for the position of authority one may possess coupled with a realization of the responsibility that goes with it are key in quality motivation of business and life.

CHAPTER 4

John *"Truth"*

*"Jesus said to him, "I am the Way, the Truth, and the Life.
No one comes to the Father except thru Me."" John 14:6*

T HE LATE COUNTRY SINGER JOHNNY Cash once recorded a song, "What is Truth?" If you ever have a chance to hear it, I think you will find it thought provoking to say the least.

Society today has taken truth and came up with so many different definitions it appears truth is whatever anyone is most comfortable with at the time.

So, what has caused one of the most basic tenants of Christianity to be defined in such a variety of ways with many times no similarity?

Scholars debate whether truth and honesty are the same. We teach our children to always tell the truth. We have citizens swear under oath in court testimony every day to tell "the truth and nothing but the truth."

We as a society have become accustomed to saying and doing pretty much whatever we need to in order to get what we want. There's a saying "the end justifies the means," which unfortunately in many areas of our society drowns out "thou shalt not lie."

Values systems are not a priority in many portions of our society today. Being truthful is not a primary value we either embrace or encourage.

Mistrust of our political system, our government and law enforcement are the result of the truth being discovered after the exposing of countless lies and conspiracies

We must reincorporate truth into our values system. We must restore confidence in our laws and our leadership in business, government, and the church. The only way this confidence can be reinstated is to use truth. We must use truth for what it is not look for ways to make it be what we want.

CHAPTER 5

Acts *"Encouragement"*

*"He traveled through that area, speaking many
words of encouragement to the people..."*

*"And when he had gone over those parts, and given them
much exhortation, he came into Greece". Acts 20:1-12*

E NCOURAGEMENT IS MOST LIKELY THE easiest tool of motivation. Giving encouragement begins in life as early as when a child begins to walk. Mommy and daddy standing by with arms extended cheerfully encouraging the youngster to "come to mommy" and the child reaching out and slowly stumbling but successfully taking those first steps.

Encouragement is vital in the early years of growth. A child faces many first-time challenges and encouragement is vital for his success. Of course, as the child grows and begins a school career and on into life more encouragement is needed hopefully combined with a quality values system and responsibility.

Children are not the only ones who require encouragement. The reality is we all have a need for an "atta boy" every now and then.

About a professional life I believe encouragement of any type is essential for not just the success of the employee but the business as well. There is remarkable truth in the saying, "a good employee is a happy employee."

Quality management skills are vital in the business world and the most vital skill at any management level is continually showing appreciation for work well done. Any business that is either failing or closing can look at a core reason being poor treatment of staff. Pay raises are nice but a good word goes a lot further.

Today our society is more self-centered than ever before. Many times, when I do in-services I hear employees talk about feeling like some of the equipment: only noticed when something goes wrong.

Sports personifies the importance of encouragement. One of the things I miss about coaching was the encouragement my players always gave each other after scoring a run, getting a hit or even after striking out or dropping a ball.

Encouragement is a motivator. Life needs motivation. Life needs positive reinforcement. Encouragement is the easiest and possibly most effective motivation.

CHAPTER 6

Romans *"Joy"*

"Now the God of hope fill you with all joy and peace in believing, that ye may abound in hope through the power of the Holy Ghost." Romans 15:13

"That I may come unto you with joy by the will of God and may with you be refreshed." Romans 15:32

W E DON'T HEAR A LOT written about the word, "joy," anymore other than when it is either in a television show, mentioned in the Bible, or in a Christmas song.

Joy relates to a feeling of peace and happiness. This feeling normally occurs at the birth of newborn babies, weddings and anniversaries and many other celebratory events.

Today however we don't seem to express as much joy in our lives as in times gone by. Whether this is the result of stress related events or either it's just part of what I refer to as the "unhappy culture," which is how I describe the attitude of many people who seem to always find something to complain about during their waking hours.

One of the motivational drills I like to use in my classes is going around the room asking each person to tell the group something they are happy about in their life at that moment and also say something good about themselves. Sometimes it takes a few minutes for each to think about it but one after another everyone says something.

From the very first psychology class I ever took one constant has always been present up until this day: people are in general hesitant to admit they are joyous or happy about anything and more reluctant to say something good about themselves in front of others.

I tend to believe most people have been conditioned over their lives to not be boisterous about themselves as it is looked at in many parts of society as arrogant. I also think there is a lack of self-confidence we all share but to many it also involves a lack of positive self-esteem that has been nurtured by their environments.

Expressing joy is indeed the most fulfilling and intrinsically rewarding feeling any individual can experience. We must strive to condition our children, grandchildren, friends, and co-workers to one of life's greatest treasures: understanding, appreciating, and expressing joy.

CHAPTER 7

1 Corinthians *"Love"*

*"Let everything you do be done in love; let all your things
be done with charity. 1 Corinthians 16:14*

I OFTEN SAY "LOVE" IS THE most powerful word in the English language. Love automatically brings a smile to our faces, happiness to our conscience and a feeling of peace and contentment.

Unfortunately, in today's world we have not let love be the primary factor in what drives us as human beings.

Keep in mind love is intrinsic. Love is not materialistic. For love to work it must come from your heart. Love cannot be stolen; it can't buy friends or buy big homes and fancy cars.

For love to be effective it must be given freely. Love is not a tool to be used for deceit, corruption, or vengeance. Many have tried to achieve personal gain under the disguise of love but never with success.

It's accurate to say Jesus had a loving and caring heart. If we have invited Jesus into our hearts it is impossible to treat people any other way but with love. Additionally, if we have accepted Christ, we will not want to disguise with false facts of love what we are doing for our own benefit.

When you let everything, you do for others be done in charity and love you are giving from the heart and pleasing God.

CHAPTER 8

2 Corinthians *"Weakness"*

"And He said unto me, 'My grace is sufficient for thee: for My strength is made perfect in weakness.'" 2 Corinthians 12:9

TAKING A PERIODIC SELF-INVENTORY IS a project I give to every client or student. It's a process that I think we should all do at the very minimum annually.

Practicing what I preach I also take a self-inventory which shows me not only the good things I've been able to accomplish but the failures as well.

Honestly, I do learn more from the mistakes and the problems I deal with in life than the good things and I try hard not to make the same mistakes again.

How we deal with problems, difficulties and challenges we face in life identifies our character and our faith.

There is nothing wrong with having weakness. We are all weak in one area of our lives or another. The key to dealing with weaknesses is to realize we have them and not let our life be limited by finding ways to overcome them.

So why shouldn't we have weaknesses? We are human. Human beings are imperfect. Human beings make mistakes, get in trouble, second-guess themselves and need help getting their lives back on track.

What we need to realize is that helping us through our adversities and turmoil is what God likes to do. What He likes even more is for us to ask Him for help. Asking God for help in times of trouble and difficulty shows our faith and belief in Him.

There is always an opportunity for God to help us and show His strength in our lives and likewise it is an opportunity for us to show the strength of faith, belief and trust we have in Him.

CHAPTER 9

Galatians *"Communications"*

*"Let him that is taught in the word communicate unto him
that teacheth in all good things." Galatians 6:6*

Without communication there can be no motivation. Indeed, without communication there also can be very little success either in business or life.

Having worked in both private and public employment I have had the opportunity to see and complete many employer satisfaction questionnaires and one area always rated is communication: how effective is the flow of information from top level management down.

Lines of communication which are either not sufficient or nonexistent are what cause relationships to dissolve. Marriages have certainly suffered because of poor communication but also relationships between parents and children. Businesses crumble due to poor communication and history is full of instances where wars have resulted because of insufficient communication.

Communication is key to motivating others. People feel important and valued when they are "in the loop." Self-esteem is high and people work harder when they feel they are part of the picture.

Good communication with others is a great way to motivate. When you communicate with others you are respected and valued. You become a vital part of others' lives when you provide accurate information that can be depended on.

CHAPTER 10

Ephesians *"Facets of Forgiveness"*

*"But God, who is rich in mercy, for His great love
wherewith he loved us...". Ephesians 2:4*

MERCY IS DEFINED AS KIND and compassionate treatment: a disposition of the forgiving and kind.

We hear about mercy in many facets of life. We hear how justice should be administered with mercy. There are many stories in history about winning wars and taking no mercy on those who had lost. Also, we see many people in our society, who are less fortunate, financially broke, homeless, sick; it is these we are asked to have mercy on their situations and give them assistance.

Mercy also involves forgiveness. Many times, in life we are asked to show mercy and forgive those who have wronged us, our families or society.

Mercy is a characteristic of maturity; it is also a characteristic of success. Mature and successful people move forward in life by not holding grudges, focusing on the future, and forgiving the past. These are individuals who don't necessarily forget but they forgive, show mercy not just to those who have caused them heartache and trouble but also show mercy to their own souls by not dwelling on the past and letting it continue to restrict their lives.

I like to think of mercy as a form of motivation. There's very little that can motivate a person more, build positive self-esteem and character, than a clear conscience, freedom from hate and revenge, being kind to others as well as wanting the best for all.

Lastly it's important to note that when you do show mercy and kindness to others you are motivating them as well. Showing mercy, forgiveness and being kind motivates people to try harder, to move forward, build their self-esteem and their character to one day return that mercy to others where needed.

CHAPTER 11

Philippians *"Virtue"*

".....if there be any virtue and if there be any praise,
think on these things...". Philippians 4:8

Virtue is a motivating word describing a worthy quality within people which draws others to want to be around them. It personifies a kind of moral excellence we should always try to achieve.

I'm not so sure we stress the importance of virtue, values, and decency in our lives today. One of the prominent attitudes in our society now is the "win at any cost," attitude: Do what you have to do and say what you have to say to get what you want and then just say you're sorry to whoever you may have offended.

People of virtue, who not only talk about quality values, but live by them are motivating and inspirational and should be magnified in our culture.

Living a life of integrity, honesty, kindness and basic compassion for your fellow man is a model of virtue we all as parents should spend our lives trying to instill in our children.

We as a society have an obligation to develop and nurture future generations of not only successful and goal-oriented individuals but also of highly motivated and educated people who incorporate their career lives with virtue, values and morality they routinely practice in their personal lives.

CHAPTER 12

Colossians *"Positive Reinforcement"*

"That their hearts might be encouraged, being knit together in love, and unto all riches of the full assurance of understanding, to the acknowledgement of the mystery of God, and of the Father, and of Christ." Colossians 2:2

ENCOURAGEMENT AND MOTIVATION CAN SOMETIMES be used interchangeably depending on the situation.

Actually I believe encouragement is a positive motivating tool within itself. Positive encouragement begins as early as birth when parents make all those weird faces and sounds at their newborn trying to get a reaction.

Positive reinforcement for good deeds done, for the anticipation of those deeds yet to be done, are both forms of encouragement.

I believe the encouragement of others to positive directions in life is a critical method for producing a successful society. Not only encouraging individuals but also teams, companies and even nations to move directions does make a difference in our life.

Encouragement like many other well-intentioned acts can be and is used for motivating negatives as well as positives. We all know there are many who encourage for their own benefits and personal agendas. Manipulation by people mixing deceit with encouragement can make others believe they are doing something for one reason when in reality the outcome is for something totally different.

As much as we enjoy the feelings of support by the encouragement of others, we also need to be aware of the intent. There's a fine line between pessimism and negativity. It does benefit to be cautious as we go through life not just agreeing to anything because of encouragement; however, taking encouragement and moving forward in positive ways for positive reasons is motivation for a more successful life.

CHAPTER 13

1 Thessalonians *"Respect Motivates"*

"And we beseech you, brethren, to respect them which labour among you, and are over you in the Lord, and admonish you...." 1 Thessalonians.

H OPE IS THE STRONGEST MOTIVATION, but most likely respect is a close second.

Respect motivates personal relationships, marriages, friendships, business deals, and national and international relations.

In any given scenario requiring cooperation and communications no success can be achieved without mutual respect.

Most marriages that end in separation or divorce are caused by lack of respect. It is my belief that although love is what binds couples together mutual respect is the glue.

Good leadership principles all revolve around respect. Studies have shown that companies where employees' opinions and thoughts are considered part of the overall mission are successful because of the mutual respect of staff and management.

Respect shows caring. People like to be cared about. People like and appreciate knowing others care for them: their safety, their health, their opinions, their ambitions and their emotional state of mind.

To respect others is to motivate them. To be respected is to be motivated by others.

CHAPTER 14

2 Thessalonians *"Charity"*

"We are bound to thank God always for you, brethren, as it is meet,
because that your faith groweth exceedingly, and the charity of every
one of you all toward each other aboundeth;" 2 Thessalonians 1:3

C HARITY IS NOT JUST AN act of kindness but a motivator to everyone to be kind and caring toward others.

Charity is the core foundation to mankind's concern for its fellow man.

Over the years, history has recorded countless acts of people helping each other throughout the world in times of extreme emergency and need.

Project CARE is an international charitable organization that aids in poverty regions of the world: disaster relief, food and nutrition education and health clinics.

The American Red Cross provides disaster relief across the United States for tornado, hurricane, flood and fire victims when needed.

But charity is also the many civic clubs and lodges such as the local Rotary, Kiwanis, Masonic and motorcycle clubs which raise money for Christmas and other holidays and the thousands of church outreach programs around our country.

The most important part of charity however is where it originate: from within our hearts and souls. Charity is a privilege we all have the opportunity at one time or another to give each other.

A person does not have to be rich to extend a helping hand and neither does one have to be poor to graciously accept help from another.

Finally, it's important to note that doing something for someone else just makes you feel good. Charity motivates both those receiving as well as those giving. We need to be grateful we can all be charitable and realize the blessing it is.

CHAPTER 15

1 Timothy *"Willing to Share"*

"That they do good, that they be rich in good works, ready to give, willing to share." 1 Timothy 6:18

SHARE: A PART OR PORTION belonging to, distributed to, contributed by, or owed by a person or government.

If you are a sibling you have no doubt heard your parents say, "share" with your brothers or sisters at one time or another.

Sharing has been looked at in life as a way to get things done. When I was a councilman our village had shared service agreements with the city for security, fire and utilities. Many communities throughout the country do shared service agreements each year building on cooperation and goodwill.

Sports is another area where sharing is primary. "Don't be a ball hog!" How many times have you heard that comment? "Pass the ball," "Play as team!," All these phrases and some not suitable to print are heard at sports events across the country every year.

In what appears by many to be a culture of "all about me," sharing seems to take a backseat. Individualism has made a severe break in the attitude of sharing.

The idea of sharing motivates and stimulates the self-esteem of all parties involved. Sharing means someone needs you or wants you to be part of something with them. You feel and are important to people willing to share with you. If you are the one wanting to share there is a feeling of reaching out and helping others and if you are the one being shared with you have a feeling of importance and that you are needed and wanted.

Sharing brings us together. It opens fellowship opportunities and it motivates all involved to build on their self-esteem and confidence.

CHAPTER 16

2 Timothy *"Controlling Yourself"*

*"For God hath not given us the spirit of fear; but of power,
and of love, and of self-control." 2 Timothy 1:7*

S ELF-CONTROL IS WHAT SEPARATES ANIMAL from man, sane from insane, maturity from immaturity.

Positive motivation, although vital in a successful life, can only be effective if those being motivated have self-control.

Being able to successfully control one's emotions, actions and thoughts on a constant basis is not easy and also not something most of us can do.

What separates maturity from immaturity is how the individual manipulates self-control. For sure there are times we all like to "let our hair down," have fun, and just relax and forget the problems of the day. That is normal and necessary for our very sanity; the problem comes when we forget our principles, morals and values going further than we should and creating some very dangerous consequences.

I think it's important to point out that self-control is just that: controlling thoughts, words and actions of yourself. Self-control is not acting like others or becoming "one of the gangs." That is not self-control but peer control or as I call it "gang" control.

Sacrificing your principles and values by acting like those in groups you have an infatuation with just to be "one of the gang," is careless and dangerous: it is anything but self-control but rather just irresponsible and in some cases irreversible.

CHAPTER 17

Titus *"Fidelity"*

"Not purloining but shewing all good fidelity; that they may adorn the doctrine of God our Savior in all things." Titus 2-10

W HEN YOU SPEAK ABOUT FIDELITY three words that immediately come to mind are loyalty, allegiance and trust.

It's safe to say the majority of us are loyal and trusting to certain people in our lives. Sometimes most of those people are either family members or life-long friends.

The most damage to be caused in any relationship is by betrayal. Betrayals come in many ways depending upon the nature of the relationship in which they are involved.

Fidelity in any relationship binds all parties. Christians have developed a spiritual fidelity with God. God's love is the cement that bonds Him with his followers.

Marriages are bonded by the pledge of fidelity as are friendships between life-long friends.

There is also a form of fidelity among siblings. The old saying, "blood is thicker than water," has more truth in it than some believe.

A final point about fidelity. Loyalty, allegiance, and trust do not require nor, is it expected that they require, no disagreements. Disagreements will always occur because no two people are alike. Fidelity is the tool that resolves those disagreements and keeps relationships strong.

CHAPTER 18

Philemon *"Be Refreshed"*

"For we have great joy and consolation in thy love because the hearts of the saints are refreshed by you brother." Philemon 1:7

B EING REFRESHED AND BEING MOTIVATED have much in common. Refreshed is like having your personal battery recharged. Motivation is the electrical current that recharges your battery.

Throughout life there comes many times when we need to be refreshed. We need to have a shot of adrenaline to get us moving again.

We all experience various highs in our life. Things are going well, the kids are getting good grades, marriage is great, and you have a good job. Then there are times when we feel like the bottom is falling out; loss of job, marital issues and children rebelling.

I believe we never appreciate the best until we start experiencing the worst. Those are the times we need to refresh our lives, step back, take a deep breath and make up our minds what's important.

Re-evaluating life is a great way to refresh and motivate yourself. There are many ways to refresh oneself. Praying, meditation, jogging, going fishing or just spending time with those you are closest to.

No matter how you do it, refreshing one's life, resetting or just getting back on track in life is a crucial motivational tool.

CHAPTER 19

Hebrews *"Run with Endurance"*

"....let us run with endurance the race that is set
before us, fixing our eyes on Jesus.."
Hebrews 12:1-2

W E CAN MOST LIKELY LOOK at endurance as a biproduct of motivation. Many projects or goals can be only accomplished through enduring hours, days or even years of struggles and obstacles. The pot of gold at the end of the rainbow can take a long time to reach and the ride isn't always easy.

People who have achieved many health related goals such as recovery from active addiction, weight loss or cancer treatments will tell you the endurance they needed to survive made the journey appear impossible but for the grace of God pushing them forward.

My father was an amputee who suffered from diabetes. The endurance he displayed while recovering from the surgery and then the therapy required to be successful wearing a prosthesis was stressful but rewarding to him as many never knew he had anything wrong when he was able to regain his normal life activities.

There are countless stories of individuals who have endured brutal childhoods of neglect and abuse to become outstanding parents and productive citizens.

The ability to endure struggles and conflict, often from within we, to eventually achieve that evasive goal, comes from the ability to motivate self, either spiritually or with smaller subgoals. It is the inner motivation and desire to beat the odds and win the fight against ourselves that brings personal satisfaction and peace of mind.

The ability to endure is sparked by our motivation from within ourselves to move forward in the race of life, keep our eyes focused on the prize and achieve both external and internal success and contentment.

CHAPTER 20

James *"Peacemaker"*

"Now the fruit of righteousness is sown in peace
by those who make peace." James 3:18

To be considered a "peacemaker" should be considered a great compliment.

The dictionary says a peacemaker is someone who brings about peace by reconciling adversaries. Unfortunately, throughout our history peace may be the most sought-after goal never achieved.

Sometimes the conditions for peace between two or more parties are virtually unattainable. Peace settlements require "give and take" between all sides involved. Peace also involves honesty and trust. It's incredibly difficult to get people who in many cases want to fight to the death to even set down to talk let alone give up something to quit fighting. How can you trust someone who is trying to kill you? How can you believe anything that person will even say?

Our world has no doubt been blessed with the strategic placement of peacemakers throughout history.

Mahatma Gandhi, Leo Tolstoy, Martin Luther King, Jr., and many others have helped or created peaceful resolutions to important crises of this world at different times in our history and in different places throughout the world.

Although we tend to think of peacemaking to between two different people, countries or races, it's just if not more, important to make peace within ourselves. The struggle to find peace within we are on-going, intense, and even fatal at times.

Many reasons for finding internal peace occur with alcohol, drugs, violence, and suicide. It's fair to say that regarding those situations, many times there is less than a desired result.

Professional counseling, both clinical and pastoral, have a more structured and positive outcome in helping find the causes for uncertainty and pain from within ourselves. I often tell people I counsel that to find a peaceful and productive life the conflicts from within themselves must be settled first.

Isn't it possible, as it says in Matthew, Chapter 5, "Blessed are the peacemakers for they will be called the sons of God," that the peacemaker should first make peace with himself?

CHAPTER 21

1 Peter *"Being Born Incorruptible"*

"Being born again, not of corruptible seed, but of incorruptible, by the word of God, which liveth and abideth forever." 1 Peter 1:23

E NGLISH TEACHERS WILL TELL US incorruptible is an adjective describing something or someone: being morally right and not subject to decay.

I like to use the word incorruptible as a motivational term describing the purity and well thought out decisions people make that lead toward a meaningful and successful life.

We have to keep in mind that morality and integrity play greatly in a productive life. In order to motivate others sincerity about the cause of why and knowledge that you are being motivated for the "right" reasons and not for some ulterior motives make all the difference in the world as to whether any motivational techniques are effective.

We as human beings are sometimes weak. We are going to make mistakes and certainly susceptible to making decisions that although made with good intentions are just wrong or we sometimes make deliberate decisions designed to manipulate or hurt others for personal gain.

It's vitally important that as we go through life we not only need to be self-motivating for our own success but we also should want to motivate our family and friends. It's crucial you motivate others as well as yourself for the "right" reasons and not for personal gain. Don't be deceptive but be incorruptible.

CHAPTER 22

2 Peter *"A Promise-Proof of Character"*

"The Lord is not slack concerning His promise as some men count slackness; but is long suffering to us-ward, not willing that any should perish, but that all should come to repentance." 2 Peter 3:9

I T'S FAIR TO SAY THAT a promise is the best proof of an individual's character; not so much the promise itself but whether it is kept or not.

Promises are motivating forces for other people, organizations as well as nations. Whether promises are kept is the deciding factor in relationships and can make the difference between trust and deceit.

We have often heard the saying, "promises are made to be broken." The sad commentary on much of our society today is that saying prevails.

The making and keeping of promises is crucial for any type of healthy relationship, be it personal or professional.

The importance of promises is an indication of the values system of those making the promises. Business, industry, and world events have all been affected over the years by either the ability to keep promises or failure to follow through with the agreement.

It's important to remember that circumstances change and in today's world change is a constant. Legitimate circumstances, not deliberate deception can and does alter some promises. Those situations need to be dealt with by both parties immediately and not left to fester. Mature parties on both sides of the promise will make the necessary alterations to continue moving forward.

Additionally we need to remember that as human beings we are imperfect and we are going to "mess up" every once in a while. Honest mistakes happen to honest people. The way promises are not fulfilled as quickly and efficiently as expected may very well be innocent. How you recognize what appears initially as a broken promise reflects your character.

CHAPTER 23

1 John *"Compassion-Caring"*

*"But whoso hath this world's good, and seeth his brother has
need, and shutteh up his bowels of compassion from him,
how dwellth the love of God in him?" 1 John 3:17*

COMPASSION IS A HOPE ALL parents want their children to have.
Compassion is a quality mature and successful people have.
Compassion is a quality those of us who are Christians and those who
are not should have.

Caring for your fellow man is to be admired and respected. I have
spent much of my life working with various charity causes, not because I
want a pat on the back but because my parents always instilled in both me
and my brother Jerry to not be selfish, to share and help others whenever
we could.

Compassion for others is a part of having a quality values system.
Having compassion for others is not just involving the giving of money. I
like to look at compassion as giving people the benefit of the doubt.

Immediate accusations are anything but compassion. For certain there
are people who take advantage of compassionate people. Unfortunately,
some have lost their lives trying to be compassionate to others appearing
hurt or in jeopardy only to be brutally taken advantage of by those very
people while offering help.

Although a sad commentary it is important to take notice of the entire situation for your own safety before offering aid or assistance and couple that notice with common sense.

Compassion, caring for others, consideration of people's situations, are qualities we need to nurture in our values system.

One other thing about compassion: give yourself some compassion. We as human beings are our own hardest critics. Being a perfectionist is one thing, becoming a neurotic is another thing. Give yourself a break occasionally. Take some time to forgive yourself.

CHAPTER 24

2 John *"Obedience"*

"And this is love: that we walk in obedience to his demands. As you have heard from the beginning his command is that you walk in love." 2 John 1:6

O BEDIENCE FROM OTHERS IS THE motivation those in leadership positions have from compliance of their instructions or directions.

God is pleased when we are obedient to His word. Parents are happy when their children are obedient to their instruction. And of course, those of us who have pets are thrilled when they are obedient.

As obedience is a motivator it is a motivator that should be used with care and responsibility.

Obedience is also a motivator for avoiding punishment. Obeying our laws and social norms motivates us to follow established procedures both legal and traditional for a more healthy and productive life.

Obedience can be looked at today as a form of social or peer pressure. Social pressures can be extreme in causing people to become obedient to current norms and to be the reason for values and behavior change.

Leadership is not a duty it is a privilege. Good leaders respect their positions and look at them as an honor. When you ask people to follow you and do as you want to remember they are being obedient because they respect you, so you need to be obedient with respect to them.

CHAPTER 25

3 John *"Prosper in Health and Soul"*

"Beloved, I wish above all things that thou mayest prosper and
be in health, even as thy soul prospereth." 3 John 1:3

THERE IS NO DOUBT THAT if we could have one wish for all mankind it would entail, "being healthy, successful, safe and prosper."

Doing well and improving throughout life is the ultimate hope we have for our children. Growing emotionally, physically and spiritually is prospering and for those we love and care about there is nothing more important we want for them.

It's fair to say that for most of us while we may prosper in certain areas of our lives the exact opposite is true in other areas.

We all know that prosperity can be the result of intense focus and work in some parts of our lives while either placing little if any interest in other parts. How many people do you know who have successful careers, beautiful home, but marriage is a wreck and kids are wild?

Prosperity isn't always universal in life. Life needs balance; tipping the scales in one direction or another can turn prosperity into disaster.

In order to have a prosperous life equal attention needs to be paid to all areas of life and there needs to be a underlying concern not to ignore or neglect other areas.

Go forth and prosper. As you prosper remember a quality life is a prosperous life, and a prosperous life is a life of values and love.

CHAPTER 26

Jude *"Satisfaction"*

"Remember that in the last times there will be scoffers whose purpose in life is to satisfy their ungodly desires. They are the ones who are creating division among you. They do not have God's spirit in them." Jude 1:16-18

I S IT SIMPLY ENOUGH TO live in a life where you are satisfied? Is satisfaction with life a goal or just enough?

I tend to believe we look at being satisfied as an excuse for trying to be better. We let satisfaction give us an excuse to not move forward to more challenging but rewarding goals.

In my school days I remember falling into that very trap. All I needed to "get by" was a "C." It required much less work, effort and time. Sure an "A" would be nice but if a "C" got me the only result I needed to pass; well guess why I never made many honor rolls.

To many times in life we let ourselves be satisfied as opposed to persevering to a more beneficial outcome. For sure circumstances do dictate how we prioritize our goals in life. Money, health and family have caused all of us to at one time or another alter our goals and plans. Life has a tendency to get in our way as we maneuver through the years.

I want to be clear that I'm not saying just being satisfied is a bad thing. In fact, many times it is the practical and responsible thing to do, but I urge you not to let simple satisfaction be a convenient excuse to deprive yourself of a happier life.

CHAPTER 27

Revelation *"Alpha and Omega"*

"And he said unto me, it is done. I am the Alpha and Omega,
the beginning and the end. I will give unto him that is athirst
of the fountain of the water of life freely." Revelation 21:6

THE ALPHA AND OMEGA, THE beginning and the end: Certainly one of the more well-known sentences in the Bible.

When you think about the beginning and ending of anything you can't help but wonder about the middle or the story itself.

When it comes to our lives are we happy with what's between the beginning and end of our lives, our Alpha and Omega?

My goals in my books as well in class and group lectures all center around motivation and values for successful living. I've spent my career working with people young and old, many successful and many not so fortunate, helping them develop their stories.

I always try to convince people to build their lives around strong morals and a healthy values system. If you use those two basic components there is good opportunity for a successful and productive life.

So when we think about the Alpha and Omega of our life it's really what's in the middle, our story, that is most meaningful. We need to impress on our children as early as possible the importance of being fair and honest with others, treating people as you want to be treated, and show genuine compassion and respect to both those you agree and disagree with.

The Alpha and Omega, the beginning and end no doubt is an important part of our lives but the story, our legacy, is the middle, the bigger story.